What Animals Eat

OMNIVORES

James Benefield

raintree
a Capstone company — publishers for children

Raintree is an imprint of Capstone Global Library Limited, a company incorporated in England and Wales having its registered office at 7 Pilgrim Street, London, EC4V 6LB – Registered company number: 6695582

www.raintree.co.uk
myorders@raintree.co.uk

Edited by James Benefield and Amanda Robbins
Designed by Richard Parker
Picture research by Svetlana Zhurkin
Production by Helen McCreath
Originated by Capstone Global Library Ltd
Printed and bound in China

ISBN 978 1 406 28912 1
18 17 16 15 14
10 9 8 7 6 5 4 3 2 1

British Library Cataloguing in Publication Data
A full catalogue record for this book is available from the British Library.

Acknowledgements
We would like to thank the following for permission to reproduce photographs: Dreamstime: Heiti Paves, 23 (sap); Minden Pictures: Konrad Wothe, 22; Newscom: Visual&Written/Kike Calvo, 11, ZUMA Press/Anthony Bannister, 19; Shutterstock: Aleksey Poprugin, back cover (right), 9, 23 (claws), arek_malang, 4, Bogdan Ionescu, 23 (algae), CreativeNature.nl (mealworms), back cover, 23, Danny Wang, 15, Dmitry Maslov, 17, Eduard Kyslynskyy, 8, 13, Galyna Andrushko, cover, hin255, 18, Igor Petrovich Potapov, 7, Ivonne Wierink, 20, Monkey Business Images, 16, Pavel K (footprints), through-out, philippou, 5, Ralph Loesche, 23 (forest), Svet-lana, 10, Vasily Vishnevskiy, 14, Vlue, 23 (root), warmer, 21, Wild At Art, 6; SuperStock: Biosphoto, 12.

Every effort has been made to contact copyright holders of material reproduced in this book. Any omissions will be rectified in subsequent printings if notice is given to the publisher.

Contents

Some words are shown in bold, **like this**.
You can find them in the glossary on page 23.

What do animals eat?

You need to eat the right food to live and grow. Animals need the right food, too. Different animals eat different things.

Omnivores eat both plants and meat.
Carnivores only eat meat. Herbivores only
eat plants.

What is an omnivore?

Omnivores are animals that eat many kinds of meat, such as insects, birds and fish. Brown bears live near rivers to catch fish to eat. They also eat berries.

Omnivores eat food from plants, such as fruit, vegetables or grains. Chipmunks eat insects but also food such as seeds.

How do omnivores get food?

Omnivores eat different things, so they have different ways to get food. A pig has a strong sense of smell, which helps it to find food.

Look at the **claws** on this hedgehog. These claws help it dig through soil to find food, such as insects or **roots**.

How do omnivores eat food?

Omnivores need different types of teeth. This raccoon has some sharp teeth to tear meat. The sharp teeth also help it to catch its food.

But omnivores need the right teeth to eat plants, too. These are flat teeth. They help omnivores to grind their food.

Are omnivores predators or prey?

Omnivores that hunt animals are called predators. Omnivores that are hunted are called prey. Which animal is the predator in this picture?

An omnivore can be both predator and prey.
For example, a mouse eats plants and insects.
But a cat might eat this mouse.

Omnivores all around

Omnivores are everywhere, including in the air. Many birds are omnivores. A woodpecker eats insects and also drinks **sap** from trees.

There are omnivores in the sea, too. Crabs are omnivores that spend time in the sea. Crabs eat **algae**, but they also eat worms.

Can you find an omnivore in your home?

The omnivore you know best is you! A lot of people eat both meat and vegetables.

Rats are omnivores that some people keep as pets. They eat fruit and vegetables, but also meaty treats such as **mealworms**.

Omnivores in danger

The cassowary's home in Australia is in danger. It lives in **forests**, but humans are cutting some of the trees down. This makes it hard to find food.

The armadillo lizard has a special way to stop being eaten. It can roll up into a ball. Its shell makes it hard for predators to eat it.

Dangerous omnivores

Some omnivores are dangerous. Flies eat lots of things from old fruit to poo! This can spread germs to other animals.

This slow loris is an omnivore that makes poison. It makes the poison in its arms. It licks the poison before biting its predators.

Omnivores are all different

Some omnivores are predators, some are prey and some are both. They all look different, but this opossum has things that many omnivores have.

Eyes that can see predators all around but also prey in front

sharp teeth

grinding teeth

claws

Picture glossary

algae
plant-like seaweeds. Crabs eat algae.

claws
hard, pointy and curvy ends to an animal's finger or toe

forest
large place with lots of trees, and bigger than a wood

mealworms
tiny, newborn worm-like animals which grow up into meal beetles

root
underground part of a plant that uses water and goodness from the soil

sap
sticky, sugary water that comes out of trees and plants

Find out more

Books

Rapping About What Animals Eat, Bobbie Kalman (Crabtree, 2012)

What Animals Eat (Kingfisher Readers), Brenda Stones (Kingfisher, 2012)

Website

education.nationalgeographic.com/education/ encyclopedia/omnivore/?ar_a=1

This site has beautiful pictures of omnivores.

Index